Cracking Social Media

A Practical Strategy for Busy Managers

Michael D. Thompson

Copyright © 2012 Michael D. Thompson

All rights reserved.

ISBN: 1477439587
ISBN-13: 978-1477439586

1 INTRODUCTION

The latest social media platform is crying out for your attention. Self-confessed experts are hailing each platform as essential in your marketing. Marketing agencies are throwing blog posts, vouchers, billboards and sales people at your front door to make sure you're not missing out. Support agencies of all shapes and sizes are boning up on the latest help files and sharing their 'in-depth' knowledge of the channel you're not utilizing. But do you really need another social media channel? Do you need social media at all?

This book will not set out to convince you of why social media is so utterly amazing that you can forgo air and simply exist inside 'the Cloud'. Personally I am not a fan of Facebook, nor of Twitter or any other social media channel. I am a fan of building a successful business. The majority of the time that simply means making money. For others, it's creating employment. For the wealthy few it's an opportunity to fund a greater cause.

For me personally, it's making money.

Do I love social media? I used to love web design, then it was blogging, then it was social media. Tomorrow it will be something new. Social media is the latest toolset adopted by businesses to drive sales. I spend a huge amount of time on Facebook, Twitter, LinkedIn, Google+, YouTube, Vimeo, Pinterest and a dozen other social media channels but if any one of them (or all of them) ceases to fulfill my business targets then I'll simply close my account and forget about it.

Social media is undoubtedly a revolution in both web technology and consumer and business communication but building a strategy based on a single technology or worse, a single platform is a time consuming and potentially lethal threat to the existence of your business.

Over the coming pages I aim to set out in simple steps how you can develop a strategy for your business that will incorporate every social media channel, especially the channels that haven't been built yet. Take note though, this is not a theoretical plan of action or an academic study of the philosophy behind social media. It is designed as a step by step process that will take you, the non-technical, busy, business owner through the necessary steps to using the latest technology to do what you set out to do, build a business; make money.

2 THE SALES FUNNEL

The sales funnel is the foundation of all sales processes. In basic terms, it is the steps required to take someone from 'product oblivious' to 'consumer'.

Figure 1 is a standard sales funnel. Search for "sales funnel" on Google Images and you will find hundreds of variations but our basic model will suffice for now.

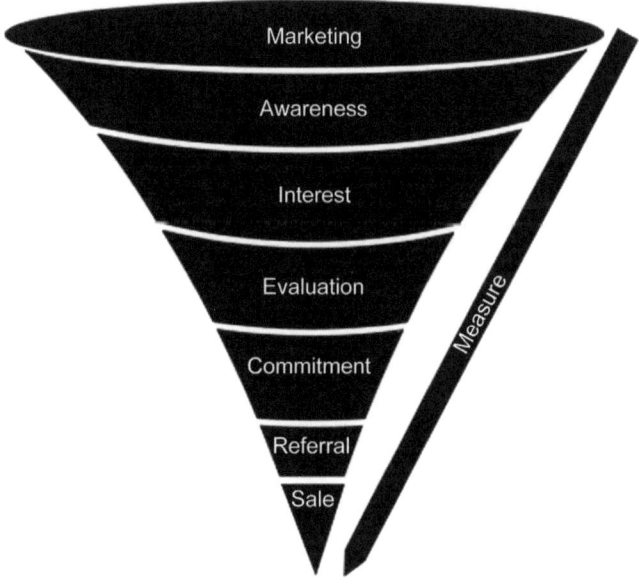

Figure 1 - The Basic Sales Funnel

Traditional marketing was a one way process beginning with marketing at the top of the funnel, reaching people through TV, radio, press, billboards, magazines, networking and so on. With sufficient levels of marketing, people became aware of the existence of a product or service and the target demographic developed an interest.

With the idea implanted, the market would evaluate the product or service against their previous experience of purchasing similar products and other products in the marketplace. This led to the innovative thinking of many companies in developing niche markets. By redefining their product outside the standard classifications they could force the market to consider their product in a new light, ultimately a light shone by the marketing department. Apple computers is a clear example of defining your own niche rather than directly competing for space. By aligning themselves with a specific demographic of user they could almost ignore the PC market and state that they are for different people. This does not change the Evaluation position in the funnel but it does set your product or service on a pedestal.

With the product or service evaluated, individuals became committed to the idea and the referral process got underway. This was the forerunner of social media when people still spoke to one another without gadgetry to assist them. As part of any buying process, especially in luxury goods, people will always seek affirmation of their choices. Affirmation takes places at several points in the buying chain including Interest, Evaluation, Referral and after the Sale. We like to know that our friends and peers approve of our choices, they understand our reasoning and look to us as someone who made the right decision. We give and seek referrals in all aspects of life but in the sales funnel it is a crucial step to moving people toward making a purchase. "Closing the sale" is covered by an endless collection of books but I can highly recommend the author Jill Konrath as someone to consider having on your shelf.

Facebook fully understands the value of the referral which is why your friend's faces appear beside everything you look at online that has a connection to Facebook. From other people's websites to the pay per click adverts running down the side of your Facebook profile your connections are appearing. Seeing someone familiar beside a new product is a powerful motivator and instant affirmation in the sales funnel.

You'll also notice that measuring occurs at every step of the funnel. Measurement is always vital in marketing and using the sales funnel model to analyse each step you take is no different. Current social media channels range from an insurmountable level of analytics through to none depending on your chosen platforms. Regardless of the numbers provided by the channel, it is essential to have a minimum level of measurement, both quantitative and qualitative but we'll cover this in more detail later.

Now that we have seen a basic sales funnel we can try to apply it to our social media channels. Figure 2 is an example of where we might fit some of the channels and their features into our model.

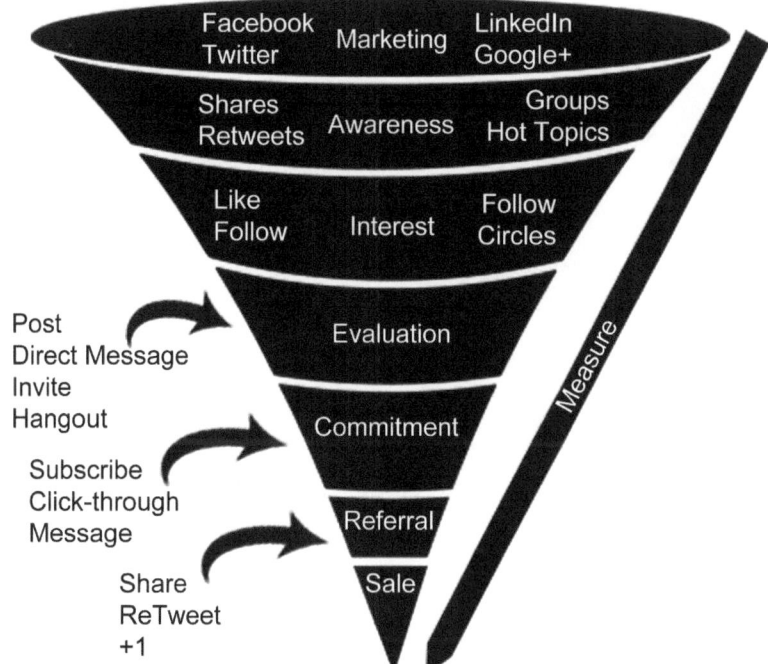

Figure 2– Social Media in a Basic Sales Funnel

While the basic idea works, there would be a fundamental flaw if we didn't change how we use the funnel. Up until now the funnel was almost exclusively within our control. When people spoke to one another about our products it was outside of our sphere of listening. Online forums and chat rooms were the nearest opportunities we had for gauging consumer sentiment but with so many websites worldwide offering these platforms it was a herculean task to monitor them. The best we could hope for was saturation with a positive message and well-timed public relations responses in the press.

The rise of social media has not only brought in the opportunity to engage directly with the consumer but from an economic stand point it has corralled our target markets into easily accessible channels. If you are starting in social media in today's market it would appear as if there is an endless list of venues we need to visit in order to engage our target market. Compared to the nineteen nineties, the platforms today are merely a handful, or two.

This doesn't help the busy manager who doesn't have time for three channels let alone twenty but let's take a look at a new sales funnel which might assist us with co-ordinating our social media toward that all important Sale.

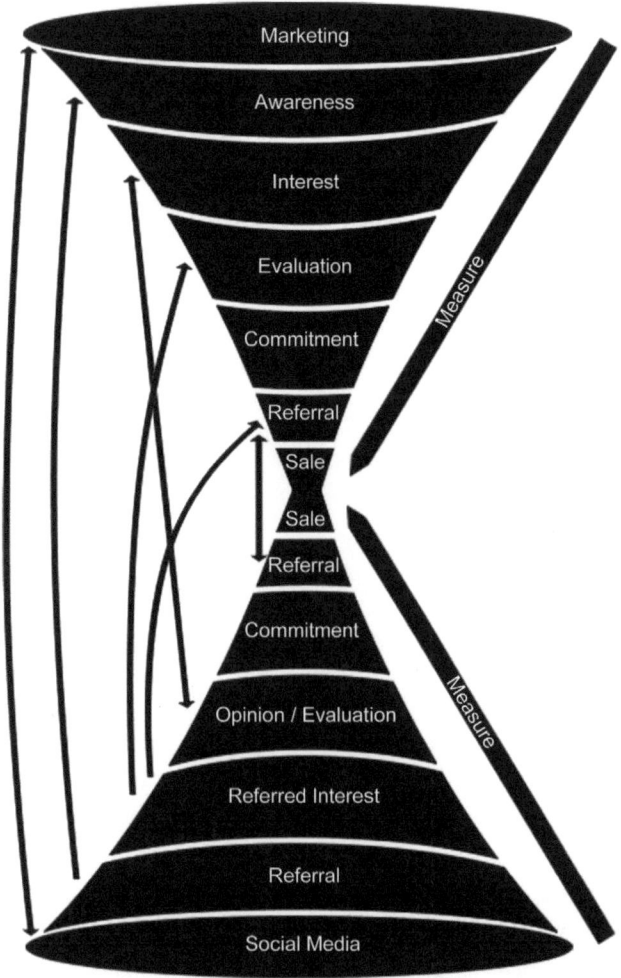

Figure 3– A New Sales Funnel for Social Media

The top half shows our standard marketing department fed funnel and the bottom is the inverse with material surrounding our brand present in the social media channels.

It's important to bear in mind that your brand may be highly active in any social media channel, regardless of your 'official presence' there. (This highlights the importance of testing each channel for your target demographic and continuing to listen even if you're not actively promoting within that space).

There are a few key differences between the top and bottom of our new funnel. While you are not in full control of the content in the bottom half, you do have the opportunity to respond directly to each section of the funnel. When someone has an opinion about your product you can reply to that opinion if they are active on your channel page. Where they are talking **about** you instead of **to** you, listening and monitoring tools will allow you to react in real time.

A very simple illustration is complaints about a faulty product start appearing on Twitter from users who don't follow your Twitter account so you can't message them directly, but you know the cause of their frustration from their posts because they mentioned your brand name in their Tweets (we'll see how to monitor your brand later). You immediately release Tweets, blog posts and Facebook updates about a 'known issue' with the item or a fix for the problem. If you know that users are highlighting similar faults in real time, where better to promote the solution than from your official brand presence on that same social media channel, even though they chose not to contact you directly. This approach by users may also say something about the perception of your customer service channels!

Another key aspect of the new sales funnel is the level of marketing being carried out for you. Referrals from the social media channels create awareness that you would have previously spent a portion of advertising money on. The Ford Motor Company are famous for bringing the Ford Explorer to market via Facebook in 2010 and generating more traffic than running a TV advert during the SuperBowl. The campaign would have taken just as much planning and preparation if not more but the final media spend was considerably less. (It is important to note the Facebook campaign was heavily promoted across multiple channels but the destination was the Facebook page.)

Referred Interest is bypassing the Interest stage and taking users straight to consideration. In sales terminology they are prequalified prospects, their friends have effectively warmed them up for a sale. At first glance this is a great leap in the marketing process, it's one less step, but if you offer a technical or complex end product your prequalified targets may be unaware of key features or requirements by not taking the time to browse all of the material you have carefully crafted to walk them through the Interest stage in the funnel. This can create a segregation of buyers who have unrealistic or uninformed expectations surrounding your services. A simple solution is keeping your product features well highlighted in documentation. Follow up e-mails and social media based downloads ensure that buyers, before, during and after purchase are fully aware of the full value of their purchase. It is also an important affirmation of the right choice in buying from you.

Interest and Opinion / Evaluation are now crisscrossing from top to bottom instantly as people write and respond to both your marketing and the material generated by others. Monitoring the opinion being generated is vital as your marketing can be cut short before it even reaches the Evaluation stage. Rather than evaluate content for ourselves we are frequently happy to take the word of the masses, especially when it includes one or two familiar faces beside a blog post. Dell made the US headlines in 2005 when pro-blogger Jeff Jarvis wrote a scathing response to the poor customer service he received after his new laptop broke down. Blog posts, news articles and social media channels quickly flooded with similar stories creating such a wealth of material that searching for "Dell" on Google returned blog posts entitled "Dell Hell" as the top results.

Even a Committed buyer is often swayed by something new and in social media channels you are only an update away from something newer, more exciting and ultimately distracting from your sale. If your product or service cannot be sold directly on a social media channel then you are in reality, going into competition with every social media channel available. With a beautiful website selling high end goods your target market will be excited to be talking about your brand and your products within social platforms. But your website isn't inside Facebook, or Google+ or Twitter, only the mention of it, in a few short words and the occasional picture. Within that post and even smaller window of time you are trying to convince your target market to leave their much beloved social media channel where their friends hang out, updates appear constantly and feedback is available 24/7. It's a big ask of any business, regardless of the writing and media production skills available to you. For a small business owner trying to write five Tweets on Monday morning it may even seem like a pointless endeavour.

The first question to ask yourself is, do I need my target market to leave their social channel? If your shop is a bricks and mortar venue with a website that merely provides more information on your stores, then your 'point of conversion' is the physical store. There is no need to compete with the unending appeal of a social media channel to get people onto your website when you can provide the same information via your social updates and profiles. Anything you can put on your website, you can put on social media platforms. Each platform can be a single stepping stone in the mind of your target market, straight to the door of your shop. If you sell online then every link is a direct connection to your shop but don't be fooled into thinking people want to see your shop entrance. If they're going to be convinced to leave a social media channel it has to be for something specific that they can receive instantly. Animated landing pages, home pages and other blockages are to be shunned at all costs. This is known as 'deep linking' in web development parlance and we'll cover it in more detail when we talk about content production.

For our physical shop owners, place the key information about your venues in every profile. When it comes to deciding what is key information in the production of any media from business cards to television advertisements we will inevitably come under the "Curse of Knowledge". Defined by Chip and Dan Heath in their book "Made to Stick", the curse of knowledge is the inability to convey even a simple idea to other people. In your head all of the information is clearly there, like giving someone map directions to your house. You can picture the twists, turns and landmarks as you describe the route but to someone unfamiliar with the road, they pick out different landmarks and perceive more or fewer twists and turns than the ones you pictured. You will have experienced this yourself while browsing the Internet. How many websites have you come across that fail to include their telephone number somewhere prominent or that they're based in a country foreign to you and therefore won't be awake for several more hours. Put together the information you think people need to contact you and be able to walk into your shop. Now give them to someone who isn't familiar with your company and ask them to complete the simple tasks of contacting you and getting to your shop. Every question they have to ask before achieving the goal is a piece of information you need to include in your profile.

Now that you know everyone who reaches your channels are equipped to make contact with your point of conversion, you need work out who those people are.

3 PEOPLE

If in doubt, start with people.

People are the foundation of everything you do. Take this statement incredibly literally. Print it in large letters and staple it to your assistant's forehead if you have to but always keep it where you can clearly see it.

Here are three examples of frequently asked marketing questions:

How can I sell more of my products or services?

How much should I spend on Internet advertising?

Which social media channels should I be on?

Taking our statement literally: "If in doubt, start with people", we can instantly answer these questions and more:

How can I sell more of my products or services?

Why would people buy (or buy more) of my products or services?

How much should I spend on Internet advertising?

How many people can I reach with Internet advertising?

Which social media channels should I be on?

Which social media channels are people using?

These may seem like obvious answers but this last answer leads us to our first big mistake by the majority of businesses I have worked with over the years. "People" is a generic term for everyone a business wants to sell to. You will rarely hear the term "people" inside a marketing agency. "Target market", "target demographic" and "engaged users" quickly replace the term "people" because "people" in relation to your business simply don't exist.

They are not a random crowd who will buy from you because you built it, sold it or even advertised it. They are a specific group of individuals who share common denominators, even if they don't realise it themselves.

The first and arguably most important job of a marketer (which in the case of many small businesses is you by the way) is to identify your target market. So forget "people" and start grouping the people who buy from you.

Step One. (Pay attention, this bit's crucial).

Make a list of the people who buy from you the most. Don't do it mentally, don't put it off, just write it down. If you're a new business then you need to examine the competition. If you operate a retail business with 'random' customers who appear to wander in off the street then geography is your first obvious common denominator but type of products sold, payment methods and even the route through your store all become potential lists.

Ultimately every business should have carried out this analysis at some point and the earlier the better but for our purposes we need common denominators which we can match to social media channels. So here is a list of four of the most popular social media channels currently being used in the United Kingdom and Ireland and their published demographics.

Social Media Channel	Published Demographics
Facebook	Country / State / Province / City Age Sex Interests (as expressed within Facebook) Connections to other Facebook pages Not connected to other Facebook pages Relationship interests Current relationship Languages Education level Workplaces
LinkedIn	Name Job Title (current and past) Company (current and past) School Locality (within country) Country Post Code Within mileage range of locality Industry Language Group membership (LinkedIn groups)* Years of experience* Job seniority level* Interested in (potential for recruitment)* Company size* Fortune 1000 listing* Recently joined (LinkedIn)* *Paid subscription required
Twitter	Interests* Location* Level of Engagement* Gender* *Advertiser account holders only
Google+	Followers

Table 1 - Social Media Demographics March 2012

Now that we know the demographic categories available from each channel, we have a list of demographics to choose from in defining our own target market.

Which of the demographics in the lists above can you fill in right away? Start with the easiest, i.e. the largest, such as Country.

Keep adding new demographics that you know right away, such as male or female, (both male and female combined is still a demographic), ages, languages, workplaces and so on. You might have a very short list to start with but out of nine billion people on the planet you'll find you've quickly narrowed it down to a few million. In the case of brand new products it's easy to believe you could sell your product to everyone in the world. Can you really afford the translation and customs costs associated with international packaging on your first day? The secret to successful selling is targeting a highly focused demographic and tailoring your marketing just to those 'people'. With that in mind we will choose our social media platforms based on highly targeted demographic marketing.

Let's draw up some example demographics from a restaurant with a website offering catering services. This is effectively two separate businesses so there will be two different sets of demographics. Consumer focused hospitality venues are notoriously well engaged through social media channels so we will concentrate on the restaurant side of the business. Remember, we're looking for the demographics to match against the social media channels so if your customers primarily order steak, it's not terribly relevant in choosing a social media channel. The content you promote on that channel will be relevant to your top selling dishes but for now we're just trying to pick a platform.

Looking at Facebook from the list above here are the demographics we can establish right away:

Country / State / Province / City – UK/County Antrim/Belfast
Age – 25-65 (the lunchtime crowd is younger than the evening folk)
Sex – male and female
Interests - eating out / wine / theatre (our venue is close to the theatre)
Connections to other Facebook pages – don't know
Not connected to other Facebook pages – don't know
Relationship interests – evenings are mostly mixed couples
Current relationship – older couples are married, younger are mixed
Languages- English
Education level – most patrons well spoken
Workplaces – lunchtime visitors must be local, primarily offices & shops

So right away we have a demographic to start comparing against the demographics of Facebook.

To work out what sort of numbers you can potentially reach on Facebook that match your demographic exactly, we have a neat trick that's completely free. Log into Facebook as you would normally (or register as yourself) tehn go to www.facebook.com/ads

Click Create and Ad in the top right corner. You will be prompted to enter a destination for your advert. Don't worry about the information you enter here, we won't actually place an advert. Type in your website address or choose your Facebook page if you have one.

Secondly, choose your brand name (not a specific post) to promote.

Next, choose a New Ad.

You will now see an audience figure on the right hand side for your potential reach. This is how many people would see your current advertisement. By default it will choose the country you are from but you can change all of these parameters throughout the page. Scroll past the advertisement section and you will see the demographics under Choose Your Audience. In these boxes enter the demographics you have picked out for your venue and watch as the number on the right changes to match your potential reach via Facebook.

Using our example above we started with 40,036,380 in the United Kingdom. Here's how the numbers focused in on our target market:

UK/County Antrim/Belfast – 251,040

Age – 25-65 – 161,760

Sex – male and female – no change

Interests - eating out / wine / theatre – this reduced our numbers below 20 so we discarded it. We know from the competition that people who eat out engage on Facebook, we just don't know how many, but if a person hasn't indicated in their Facebook profile that one of their interests is eating out in restaurants or hasn't talked about it regularly to their friends then they will not register in the interests section.

Connections to other Facebook pages – don't know

Not connected to other Facebook pages – don't know

Relationship interests – evenings are mostly mixed couples

Current relationship – older couples are married, younger are mixed

Languages- English – 91,300

Education level – we'll assume College Grad – 16,800

Workplaces – lunchtime visitors must be local, primarily offices & shops

We could list actual names of workplaces here out of interest but many people may not list where they work in their profile. It will also narrow our demographics down too far to be practical.

We have however moved from the idea that Facebook will put us in front of 900 million people to 16,800. This is a much more manageable figure in terms of engagement and sufficiently large to make it worthwhile managing a presence on Facebook.

To cancel your advert simply close the window or go to another web page.

We perform the same task on LinkedIn at www.linkedin.com/ads

This time enter a campaign title, target website, headline and description. You can enter any text at all to get to the next step.

On the next page you get all of your demographic options neatly laid out to tick the relevant boxes.

Our starting figure is 150,325,602

Our finishing figure is 2,566,787.

Unfortunately our county (state) wasn't listed within the UK so we couldn't narrow it down very far but we do know there is a good range of people we can potentially contact so LinkedIn is a real opportunity to engage.

For Twitter and Google+ there are currently no demographics available for the UK as advertising accounts haven't been opened here yet so they will remain "try it and see" accounts. We simply have to start engaging via those channels and advertising our presence on them to determine their value.

Step Two.

When we consider social media channels we automatically gravitate to the ones our friends are using, the media are pushing and the platforms we are familiar with. Are these the platforms our target demographic is using? If it's not, stop using them. Even Facebook. The size of the social media platform and its place in the global psyche is irrelevant if the people you're trying to engage with aren't on it.

The Internet is famous for many things but one of them is the ability to fail quickly. Failing is almost inevitable in business, it's part of the testing process when it comes to marketing. To limit our ability to fail we can resist change, new ideas and forward thinking. Alternatively we can define our own limits by building platforms, testing them and closing them down again if they are unsuccessful. No one wants to build a social media presence that fails, largely because 'people' will see it happen. If your target market isn't using the platform then the 'people' who saw your brief excursion on that channel are mostly irrelevant to your sales anyway.

Choose one social media channel, read the beginner's help files (every channel has them and there are some listed in the resources section at the back of this book), build a simple presence and start testing by posting comments aimed at your target demographic, i.e. engaging, even if no one is listening yet.

4 TEAM BUILDING

It's natural to want to jump in when you have a new platform, the opportunity to connect and a handful of great ideas on how to engage with your target market are always exciting to publish but should you really go right ahead and fire out your first post?

Personally I would say yes. While there are a thousand good reasons not to, like share trading, you never really understand the pressure of a live trade until you make one. It's easy to trade on a dummy account day and night convincing yourself that you're ready for live trading and that you fully understand the fear and pressure of holding a trade position overnight, until you actually do it. Real sweat clouds your judgement, you suddenly feel ill equipped and isolated no matter how many news feeds you're watching. By the time you've made your second trade you're starting to feel a little more in control but there's no getting away from that first rush when you make a live trade with real money. For that reason alone it's imperative that you get yourself into the market space and start actively engaging with your target market.

There are a few guidelines worth bearing in mind though. Start as you mean to go on. If you work in a small company it's easy to write a dozen updates today when the office is quiet but what about next week when a big order comes in? Will your page go quiet for a few days or will you just write one or two posts? Who handles complaints? Complainants may have been lurking for weeks or even months for an opportunity to contact you and suddenly Facebook has made that instant and easily accessible. If you fire out a great post you just thought of this evening and someone replies, will you be there tomorrow evening for their next query?

Having a policy is vital for all sizes of business, even just for your own peace of mind. IBM became infamous for releasing their social media policy online when readers realised it was over forty pages long. It was a behemoth of a document and completely unrealistic in terms of memory retention. Policies should be simple, concise and complimentary to your staffing policies.

Start small, divide up roles with clear rules for response types and brand guidelines. Small businesses working on the same theory that branding is for big businesses often fail to put in place brand guidelines. These can be as simple as "you are not allowed to talk negatively about the brand in public". This clearly extends to social media and therefore does not need repeating in a social media policy but that's not to say staff don't need reminding.

While your receptionist might be technically qualified to start a Twitter account, are they trained to handle product complaints or enquiries from competitors? Even if they feel qualified can they be trusted to respond in a timely matter in a public domain? Are complaints recorded off the social media platform for future reference? Customer service via social media is a double edged sword. If your staff are trained to deal with customer enquiries and they all have access to social media then it can be a great channel for fast responses. Be aware that the majority of customer service is based around problems so a separate channel might be called for. Anyone new stopping by your Google account to browse your profile will be put off by the majority of comments relating to a faulty product while you believe you're providing great service. O2 for example operate a heavily monitored customer service channel via Twitter. They also operate a separate account for talking about all the great new products and fun stuff they love to share. In this way they can separate the two and avoid muddying the water with customer service. O2 monitor their Twitter name proactively to measure brand sentiment so if you complain about their service via Twitter and include their Twitter name you will get a response from O2 asking you to follow them so they can contact you directly. I tested their response when my service was interrupted and I couldn't get a reply by telephone. Within two days I had a complaint handler addressing my query and ultimately getting it resolved after a complaint via my Twitter account.

Another area for clear policy management is etiquette. What tone of language can your social media users employ with your followers? It is important to keep your language natural. No one wants to read a press release cutting every day but swearing and text speak are automatic failures in all forms of business communication.

Each team member should be trained to use the sales funnel, especially in the content production stage. Regardless of which role they are responsible for it is vital to understand the importance of the interaction, relationship building, referral and sales processes involved in social media engagement. A carefully built level of interaction that is educating, entertaining and developing a community around your brand can be broken in a single update with a hard sell from someone who doesn't understand the culture of social media. That's not to say hard selling techniques and social media are mutually exclusive but it's key that everyone knows their roles and when they can hit the send button.

Review processes are incredibly important in social media. They are by their nature dull and soul sucking. Everyone feels under pressure to have performed and there are usually some inflated numbers rolling around. But don't let this put you off and don't be swayed by the vanity metrics either. Use real measurements (more on this later) of your current success and ensure the people you are reporting to understand the slow process of follower engagement and community building. Like networking, social media marketing is akin to farming, not hunting. Reviewing your engagement levels, target market interaction and reach will demonstrate how your content is being responded to. Content production is the highest cost in social media marketing as it is the most time consuming. Knowing what works, what feeds each portion of the sales funnel and how effective it is will give you clear direction for future production. Distributing inspiring quotes from famous people will give you an easy feed of material but add nothing new to the education of your followers about your brand, inspire them to purchase from you or entertain them for more than a second or two. The occasional quote from a figure directly relatable to your target market followed by a blog post around a product inspired by that same quote will move people through three steps and invite engagement. It's more work but it is content production that gets results and results are what we are interested in.

Where you have multiple venues and a single brand it might be easier to centralise some roles such as complaints, feedback suggestions or other specific queries. A chain of restaurants for example will have a collection of very busy managers. It will be important for every manager to know about the complaints specific to their restaurant but if desserts are made offsite and supplied by a third party vendor then product queries may be better handled by the purchasing department. This division of roles can be ascertained by a short survey to each manager asking for their top ten enquiries, five which are questions they can't answer and five which they feel they must answer personally or at least within the venue.

When it comes to setting up social media accounts you will also have to make a clear rule about who is allowed to setup a page representing your brand. An overzealous employee of one venue might feel they are qualified to build a page and speak on behalf of the brand. This is an important ruling in your policy document. Are employees are allowed to represent the brand publicly unless directly authorised? Personally I would recommend a page for each venue where people can check in at the venue. This builds a community around that location but a 'headquarters' page might also be in order where you can distribute key brand messages and 'global' updates that are applicable to all pages. It is then a requirement (as mentioned in the policy document) that head office updates must be shared on local pages. Obviously this only works if each venue has the time to manage their own accounts. It only takes one weak link and it will look like one venue is offering a poorer service simply due to its peers promoting their accounts.

Lastly, ensure you double up on every account. Many social media accounts are tied to a single personal account or email address. Provide a business email address that other people have access to so that no social media channel can be left without access when someone leaves the company, decides they no longer like your brand or simply take off sick. It is also a vital clause in your social media policy to ensure that even after leaving your employment that the person may not represent your brand in any form. Claiming an account handled by a former employee through a social media channel is a long and time consuming process and the only grounds some channels offer for reclamation is a breach of trade mark or intellectual property. Ensure that anyone with administrative access or a personal account that includes your brand name is legally obliged to stop using that account upon termination. A second administrator to block that persons access is also useful but not always available from the channel.

For more information on writing a policy have a look at SocialMedia.org. There you will find an open source document providing guidelines for best practice on developing a social media policy and what to include. The best part is, it's all in plain English: http://www.socialmedia.org/disclosure/

With your team defined and trained to at least a minimum level with a basic policy in place the next step is start working the sales funnel. Our channels are in place and we're all ready to engage with your identified target market.

5 ENGAGING YOUR TARGET MARKET

Engaging, or communicating with your target market in a meaningful way, i.e. building a relationship is very easy to do. Here is a simple example:

"Has anyone else read "Made to Stick" by Chip & Dan Heath? It's a great book on how to explain ideas."

There's not much to this example, it's simply a book recommendation, but if we break it down it ticks all the right boxes.

"Has anyone else" – Asking questions is opening up your pages to feedback. It demonstrates your channels are not all one way.

"read Made to Stick" – I could have asked a question about a film or any book in the world but I specifically chose a book about marketing, why? Because if you're reading this book then I know you already read books about marketing so it's not a hard sell to try and get some responses. The book "Made to Stick" has been around for a few years and it's quite well known. By inviting positive responses I can build rapport and comments making my social media pages look lively and interesting.

"It's a great book on how to explain ideas." – This is a personal recommendation, it demonstrates I've read the book myself and there are real individuals behind the corporate page name.

Now I'm not suggesting you break down every Tweet, update and message into clearly relatable parts but do have a think about the person you are writing to. The art of writing is a full time occupation for many professionals but the ease of quickly communicating messages has somehow left businesses ignoring the importance of crafting well written copy and simply diving in. While this may be a cost consideration, the importance of every message sent cannot be underestimated. Each line of copy released under your brand is a public relations message, a personal customer interaction and a brand message so it's important to get it right, every single time.

For this reason, for time saving and for your sanity, you need a content strategy. A simple plan of action that steers your content, inspires the next update and keeps life simple.

Many sales people will be familiar with the Art of War by Sun Tzu, a book of immense strategic thinking in assessing one's enemy, their capabilities, their numbers and comparing them to one's own position. It is written in such a way that its teachings are easily used as metaphors in business but this has led to a widespread belief that customers are your targets, not your allies. We feel pressurized by the existence of our competition and our limited budgets to assess our targets then attack them with our message for maximum impact. In the world of Social Media we must undertake an alternative approach. Authors such as A.A. Milne and Beatrix Potter are more suited to the new medium in identifying with our target markets; giving our audience short memorable prose and figures they can relate to and seek to engage with rather than heavy copy repeatedly fired from our desks.

If you are in any doubt that Winnie the Pooh is too far removed from today's society and the world of social media, here is a quote from Pooh's Little Instruction Book:

"You can't stay in your corner of the Forest waiting for others to come to you. You have to go to them sometimes."

6 WRITER'S BLOCK PART 1

It's easy to write random content for social media channels. It gives us a sense of published, like a mini author. We have a soap box to the world and on behalf of our brand we declare this space ours. Tomorrow morning when we sit down at the computer we can admire our social media flag which proudly displays our logo and our first post. Now we have no idea what to write and we don't really have the time anyway.

What we need is a content strategy. We need a resource that we can dip in and out of while at the same time feeding our sales funnel.

Starting with 'People', we will produce posts that tempt our target market. This will test the channel to prove our demographic is in there, just waiting to hear from us. Secondly it will gather in early adopters giving us the opportunity to test them with variations of content type. Here is a sample first post I have used for launching a social media channel:

"Welcome to our brand new Facebook page! Feel free to Like us, share us and join in the conversation. We hope to bring you lots of news and insights about our products and look forward to your feedback and suggestions."

This post ticks a number of boxes. It's personal, it makes it clear that our page is new (not just empty), we are inviting conversation and feedback and we are telling people why they should Like our page. When you click Like on a Facebook page it can be for a number of reasons. You want to demonstrate to your friends that you associate with that brand. In the case of Red Bull you want to tell people that you are adventurous, someone who needs energy drinks because their diary is packed. Equally you expect to receive something from that brand, useful information, entertaining media or some other emotion provoking content. Tell people what to expect and they will happily subscribe to you.

Most social media channels will walk you through the process of creating your first public post but beware that their aim is to keep you on their platform and get you comfortable using it right away. Take your time, especially where wizards are concerned. Wizards are those step-by-step walkthroughs which explain the key elements of setting up your account and making sure you have promoted yourself to your target market by the time the wizard is complete. Always skip any steps that include promoting your new page. That may sound counter intuitive but frequently our pages simply aren't ready for the public yet.

The Facebook 'Create Page' wizard is a clear example. Their wizard will walk you through creating a page, uploading a logo and telling your friends about your presence all in the space of five minutes. If your friends respond instantly they will be greeted with a blank page beside your logo.

Always complete your page construction, post an update or two that asks for interaction and sets out your message and branding first. When that is done, then you can tell your friends. Ask them for some feedback and then start to promote your social media presence. It's fast and exciting to get your presence launched and 'live' but if you create euphoria in the early stages then disappoint with a lack of content, you will lose followers forever. Follow Google's example, "better to over deliver and under promise".

With our first post out there and attracting a friend or two it's time to unleash our strategy. Create a new spread sheet with seven columns. If you would like to download a copy of the spread sheet go to www.crackingsocialmedia.net.

Date	Update	Link	Educate	Engage	Personal	Sell
02/04/2012 08:05						

In the Date column enter the date and time that you want to release your next update in the format shown. Now write your next status update in the Update column and if you are including a link, enter it in the Link box.

Think of updates that you want to release on Monday, Wednesday and Friday for example. So here's our sample sheet:

Date	Update	Link
02/04/2012 08:50:00	Monday again! What was the best thing you did this weekend?	
04/04/2012 08:50:00	To get the most from your blog make sure you share new posts on your social media pages and social book marketing sites.	
06/04/2012 08:50:00	Our latest marketing blog post is out now	http://www.cracking socialmedia.com/ marketingblog.php

Now copy the dates and times for the following week and enter your next three updates. Adjust the times to a new window of exposure. This week we're using 08:50 to capture the readers checking their social media channels just before they officially start work or are still sitting on the bus. Next week we'll try the lunchtime crowd. Don't worry about whether the updates are brilliant at this stage, just pop something in the boxes.

Date	Update	Link
09/04/2012 12:55:00	A new report from AppData show Facebook engagement rising	http://www.appdata. com/apps/facebook/ 156477574409753- facebook
11/04/2012 12:55:00	What's the biggest challenge you face in choosing a social media channel to adopt?	
13/04/2012 12:55:00	We'll be closed from lunchtime today but we're back bright and early on Monday.	

Once again repeat the above process but change the days to Tuesday,

Date	Update	Link
17/04/2012 08:50:00	E-mail is still a high engagement strategy for marketing. Use it to boost your social media exposure.	
19/04/2012 08:50:00	Something fun for a midweek boost to your happiness.	http://dilbert.com/strips/comic/2012-05-09/
21/04/2012 08:50:00	If you're reading this, the chances are your target market could be open to your updates too.	

Thursday and Saturday.

We now have three weeks of content, releasing updates three times per week. Our stats will show the level of engagement for each date and time and within just one month we will know the best time to send out updates for the best possible response. This testing and reviewing is a constant process but it gets faster and easier every time you do it. I would recommend monthly as a minimum review period.

This may have seemed like a hard process but once you have written two or three posts it starts to get easier. Within that first month everything you read and discover starts to be broken down automatically in your mind as a possible update. Before you know it you will see the world in 140 characters or less and your time to produce content will reduce dramatically.

Another debate which rises regularly is how often to release material to your public. I have heard arguments for daily, three times per week, weekly and every variation in between. In 2011 I opened multiple Twitter accounts and tested them to destruction. This simply means I built up a following of at least 100 people following each brand then released Tweets at varying frequencies.

At one update per week growth was almost zero and engagement was negligible. There was simply too little content to be seen amongst the huge stream of Twitter updates. At three updates per week growth was slow but engagement was higher with regular responders starting to appear.

With updates once per day growth increased on a weekly basis and direct replies averaged two to three times per week. Updating twice per day (morning and late afternoon) increased growth slightly but engagement levels remained the same. Finally I increased updates from twice per day to thirty per day. At ten updates per day, followers started to actively stop following the accounts and over ten updates per day started to generate complaints. By thirty updates the accounts were empty of followers.

Don't forget that Twitter can handle a lot more updates than other channels but that's not to say future channels won't suit higher volumes of content. Start with three times per week, testing for the best days and times. If your audience will permit it, increase to once per day. You will know yourself how often you want to hear about certain products. Marketing hints and tips for example are valuable every day but you don't necessarily want to think about selling over the weekend. This may simply mean Saturday is a good day to release a funny link but your followers will soon let you know verbally or with their feet if you're getting it wrong.

Luxury or occasional purchases such as furniture are less exciting and therefore won't benefit from twice daily updates but if you position your brand as a source of the innovative and interesting in addition to your own furniture offerings then you can increase your engagement levels without annoying your readership. I don't want to see the latest sofa every day on my personal Facebook page but a daily image of fun and quirky home design is acceptable with the occasional 'sale' thrown into the mix.

The next step before we relax and start unleashing our collection of posts on an unsuspecting public is to categorise each update. You will have noticed from our first table four extra columns:

Date	Update	Link	Educate	Engage	Personal	Sell
02/04/2012						

In each of these four new columns, enter the number one beside each post to categorise the type of update:

Date	Update	Link	Educate	Engage	Personal	Sell
02/04/2012	Monday again! What was the best thing you did this weekend?			1	1	
04/04/2012	To get the most from blogging…		1			
06/04/2012	Our new forum is now online	Link				1
09/04/2012	A new report from AppData…	Link	1			
11/04/2012	What's the biggest challenge…			1		
13/04/2012	We'll be closed from lunchtime today…		1			1
17/04/2012	E-mail is still a high engagement strategy…		1			
19/04/2012	Something fun for a midweek…				1	
21/04/2012	If you're reading this…		1			
Totals		2	5	2	2	2

When I read through the three weeks of updates they looked quite good but upon categorisation I suddenly realise my direct engagement levels are quite low. Education levels are high which is a good strategy as it builds your brand as a thought leader, provider of useful information and source of knowledge but our mix of posts might be slightly too heavily weighted towards education and not enough towards building a community who engage with us.

Our links total just two but in percentage terms, 50% of our links send followers away from our own content. For future updates we would be better to take the graph from our AppData.com link and enter it into a blog post which we can then invite comment around.

Let's look back at the key areas of our sales funnel and see how our content production relates to moving people through the process.

	Educate (5)	Engage (2)	Personal (2)	Sell (2)
Marketing	3			2
Awareness	1	2	2	
Interest	1			
Evaluation				
Commitment				
Referral				
Sale				

Based on the types of content we have produced we are covering the early stages of the sales funnel quite well with a good blend of content but the later stages are completely untouched. The funnel is so shaped as to encourage this ratio but we must be aware that in our second month and going forward that we need to add a few 1s to the last four stages of the funnel. The social media fed interaction coming back from our followers we discussed back in Chapter 2 will assist with this but it's not enough to rely on others to fill our funnel for us.

7 THE HOLY GRAIL OF MARKETING

If our market is seated at their computer reading about the latest amazing feats of dare devils around the world, watching baby cheetahs being born live via web cam or following the hottest gossip on their favourite pop stars then our chances of posting material so utterly dramatic that people will leave their seats or favourite social channels and rush to our point of conversion is completely unrealistic.

Thought of by many as the Holy Grail of marketing, changing a person's behaviour is an unrealistic goal of the small business owner. If you can develop a formula (or a drug) that instantly changes behaviour in the space of a Tweet (or a million Tweets) then you are on the verge of becoming spectacularly rich. (Just remember you heard it here first). If a member of your target market buys a McDonalds every Saturday morning with their family then you are not just competing with building a better breakfast menu. You are asking people to change their routine, accept new surroundings on a regular basis, change their comfortable pattern of behaviour and embrace a whole new perception. Going on holiday and trying new food is always exciting but only because we know it's temporary. If we are dropped into a Cypriot street market indefinitely we will not be able to sit down comfortably with our family and plan to come back next week. We might be tempted to try a venue out of necessity but if we see a familiar yellow M in the distance we will go there first to be assured of a familiar meal.

Our best chance as any size of business, is branding. Branding has always been for large corporations. Big businesses with big budgets spend money on branding. Brand advertising is the side of a Formula One car, sponsorship deals at international trade shows and celebrity endorsements in television advertisements. Branding is expensive, long term and really not for the small or medium enterprise. These are common misconceptions. Branding can be cheap, effective, short term and perfect for the small business. In 2004 I launched my second company, selling marine photography equipment online. It was an ecommerce site with a cosmpletely original name (i.e. unknown) and a marketing budget of one hundred pounds. I entered a large international market and using branding became the largest stockist of marine photography equipment in Ireland within one year. Social media didn't exist in the mainstream web of the UK and Ireland back then but in today's marketplace branding via social media is crucial to your business success. Every Tweet, update and post is an exercise in branding. If you're a sole trader accountant then the information you provide that assists potential customers with their records is an exercise in promoting yourself as a brand. People will come to recognise your material and you will become known for providing useful information. When your target market from within those people listening have additional questions, they will remember your posts and contact you.

Red Bull is one of the foremost exponents of branding. Have a look at Red Bull social media channels and count how often you see their physical product appear in the media they distribute. It's relatively rare. Their brand is frequently seen in sponsored events from local motorbike trials to their own record breaking stunts, most recently trying to break the sound barrier during free fall with a sky diver jumping from space. With some of the biggest and most exciting media produced why is their product not featured in every single image? Red Bull is more than just an energy drink, it represents a way of life. If you drink Red Bull it says you are part of a group of people who like adventure, take risks and push the limits of human endeavour. Red Bull's social media is a direct reflection of this. Their videos, photographs and quotes are pure adrenaline, professional and homemade extreme sports adventures but rarely do they feature the product. Admittedly, that's a lofty target for our sole trader accountant but the effect is the same. Your target market will uphold your brand in their minds as a source of information and regardless of how exciting launching yourself off a cliff in a homemade jet pack might be, people still need to file their accounts and check they are paying the right amount of tax so your message remains relevant and important.

This brings us to our second challenge, timing. Social media is frequently quoted as too time consuming and therefore not within the capabilities of a small business. Branding is a never ending process and Coca Cola demonstrates this demand on a daily basis. If we didn't need to constantly brand ourselves then the world's largest and best known soft drinks company could save a fortune on advertising. Yet they continue to hang their banners on school sports grounds, give away millions in charity support and run television advertising year round. The reason for this is timing. Coca Cola sells via the same shops as Pepsi, frequently on the shelf beside one another among numerous other colas and soft drinks. By ensuring their brand is seen by every new generation they are building brand loyalty from an early stage. They are also maintaining the loyalty of the older generations who grew up with Coca Cola as a regular part of their lives. Christmas is synonymous with the Coca Cola lorries appearing on our TVs. The lorries now appear at live events around the globe decked out with Christmas lights keeping our love of the brand alive. Personally I prefer the taste of Coca Cola to Pepsi anyway but when I plan to sit down with a movie or go to the cinema I imagine myself with a Coke, nothing else. It is always in the back of my mind, just for that moment when I decide I want a cola drink.

Social media is the perfect platform for creating that brand timing. By associating yourself with your target market, their ideals, their lives, their challenges and their fears you can build yourself into their psyche on multiple levels including emotion and memory.

Memory is important because there are so many other elements out there competing for attention which is why it's important to maintain a presence on social media, not just a page but regular updates.

Regular updates that can attach themselves to the emotional triggers are one of your most powerful tools in driving engagement from your followers. Reaching people on an emotional level creates a lasting memory and a bond that is hard to ignore. How many adverts have inspired the desire to visit a foreign country, try a new chocolate bar or be seen wearing a particular brand? It's an emotional response to a branding message.

So where do these long term memory effects and emotional triggers fit for our sole trader accountant? Over time your updates will be remembered for being useful and maybe once, crucial. That one post that solved a problem for someone will be enough for them to remember you. It may have been just another update for you but it's a vital piece of knowledge that solved a problem for someone else. As the source of that solution you will be engrained in their memory. Continuing updates will keep your name in their memory but that problem solving emotion will remain tied to the psyche without further work from you.

A frequent problem of retail stores is the competition around the products they themselves sell. If you sell Nike trainers it's unlikely you will be able to produce social media based content that inspires people to buy those trainers better than Nike can. Co-branding is a powerful tool in the marketing mix and not to be underestimated. If you are promoting a brand which will remain more powerful than your own marketing you have two non-mutually exclusive options. Defining your own niche and co-branding.

Defining your own niche as shown in our earlier example with Apple is to create an ethos around your style of sales. This is reflected in everything about your store from the logo to the layout. Hanging mountain bikes from your ceiling and placing your Nike trainers on boulders positioned on your shop floor immediately attracts people who like the outdoors, travelling, extreme sports and adventure. The Nike logo prominently displayed above the rocks creates the co-branded link between the stylish Nike commercials and your niche market for outdoor footwear.

Another key ingredient of branding is aspiration and Disney are the masters of capturing aspiration in an instant. If you're familiar with a Disney store you'll know there's more to selling a soft toy space man than simply hanging him on the wall in a shiny box. As a globally recognised character, Buzz Lightyear could be sold (and is sold) in any supermarket with little or no surrounding branding. Kids and adults alike would recognise him and make the purchase without question. But a trip to a Disney store is exactly that, it is an experience. Buzz Lightyear toys hang with space murals behind him, spaceships hang from the ceiling and stars are projected onto the walls. It is an emotional experience of fun, pleasure and even adventure as you 'explore' the aisles. Children aspire to be astronauts and adventurers. Adults aspire to making their children happy and giving them enjoyable experiences while getting value for money. Buying Buzz from a Disney store adds considerably more to the purchase than buying him from a supermarket shelf. Don't forget this vital ingredient when you develop your own branding, especially within social media channels. People aspire to many things and the products and services they purchase are a reflection of those aspirations. We don't all buy treadmills and energy drinks because we're athletes. We buy them because they make a step toward our aspiration of cover model fitness. (For some of us there are several steps required here but again the number of different fitness apparatus I own perfectly reflects the number of steps still required to reach my aspiration.)

So how does this translate into short updates on social media? When we write about our products and services we are frequently talking about the things which people aspire to. When we choose the channels we are writing in, we are targeting our demographic. Our images of treadmills on social media will feature slim, toned people who clearly haven't tasted chocolate in years but we will place those adverts in front of people who already own gym memberships but also enjoy large chocolate ice creams because we know they aspire to look like the person in the photograph but aren't there yet .

This is branding your product or service. It is more than the list of keywords we might write on the back of a business card, it is the aspirations, ideals and problem solving solutions, highlighted in a context our target market is already considering.

With today's target market now considering our product, how do we capture tomorrow's market without repeating the process from square one?

8 WRITER'S BLOCK PART 2

So what types of posts can we produce to start incorporating the next four stages? Don't think about social media and the platforms available, think about the People and the traditional models of selling. The People at the Evaluation stage are no longer just People, they are pre-qualified leads. They are engaged with your brand, followers, subscribers and readers of your content. They are open to whatever you send them and will respond to it in one way or another. Personally, if I have reached the Interest stage then a customer testimonial might move me to the next stage of the funnel. It will assist me in the Evaluation process. Special offers, free trials, consultations, workshops, events and other traditional sales techniques will contribute to moving me through the funnel and onto the Sale. As occasional updates in the mix of content that is mostly Education, Engagement and Personal I will be constantly informed about your brand, the opportunity to buy will be present in my mind and any concerns or hesitations I may have will be addressed in the blend of material fed to me.

It would be easy to believe at this stage that the process is a simplified one and with the right magic formula you will be able to drive people running to their phones and shopping carts but don't forget it's a process and requires a high level of involvement at a personal level. No matter how good your prose is, how engaging your images are or how often you release content, people will buy from people. You also have the equally pressing problem of what to write next month. To address this very problem I have made a list of over one hundred ideas for content production. When you are sitting down with your spread sheet and aiming to write one month or more of updates and your mind goes completely blank, this is the list to get you back on track.

Selling and Interaction
1. Start a discussion
2. Ask followers to sign up to a newsletter
3. Drive followers to a blog
4. Give out a special offer
5. Drive followers to your point of conversion
6. Create a second timeline dedicated to a specific event or service on Twitter
7. Create a Group on Facebook to encourage discussion & follower interaction

Videos
If you shoot a 'home video' make sure the lighting is bright and the audio is very clear or you'll do more harm than good. Amateur videos are very popular and break through the 'corporate barrier' but products, office tours, interviews and conference speeches should be assigned to professionals.

8. Virtual tour of office or production facility
9. Staff interviews
10. Products in use
11. Video preview of product
12. Product or service comparisons
13. How-Tos
    a. Innovative or unusual uses for a product
    b. Fixing faults
    c. Addressing common queries
14. Screen capture – record your computer screen with free software such as Camtasia then add a voice over
    a. Website tours
    b. Product specific web pages
    c. Tutorials – how to contact support, how to register, updating your information
15. Client interviews
    a. In-person

b. Via online conferencing, e.g. Skype. Use screen recording software to capture the interviewee then mix with video of interviewer asking questions or giving responses.

Photos

Not every photo has to be professionally taken, some images benefit from the non-professional personal touch. Staff profiles and products however should always be taken by a professional. Office birthdays, conference shots and staff playing with new products can be taken with a mobile phone, just make sure you hold it steady and turn up the lights as much as possible.

16. Staff profiles
17. New products
18. Special or little known features of products
19. Products in use from customers
20. Staff trying out products
21. Staff/client meetings
22. Board meetings
23. Conference speakers
24. Conference delegates
25. Premises
    a. Outside images help people find your venue
    b. Internal images give people an insight behind the 'corporate brand'

Links

Always remember that a link is a route **off** your platform. Use them sparingly unless they enhance your product or brand.

26. Industry news
    a. Setup Google Alerts for news stories
    b. Register on TweetBeep.com for Twitter news
27. Funny content
    a. Everyone loves 'funnies' or 'bloopers'. Make sure they're relevant and appropriate to your target market and don't over use them. "Fun Friday" or "Merry Mondays" are very popular, especially from brands not normally categorized alongside comedy

b. Comedy photos and videos, link to the original content and credit the user.
  c. Local news websites are good sources of pre-vetted material
28. Complementary products and services
  a. If a service or product adds value to yours, share that information
    i. Accountants and specialist tax advisors often work together
    ii. A cleaning product may be enhanced by use of a specific applicator
    iii. A blogger might expand on a specific area of information your website mentions in relation to its own content
    iv. Products will sell better if you provide links that educate your affiliates on how to market your product for you

Third Party Comments
29. Quotes
  a. These don't have to be industry related, just related to your target market
30. Useful quotes from an industry conference speaker
31. Client testimonials
32. Feedback – good and bad

Free Stuff
33. Desktop Wallpapers
34. Mobile Phone Wallpapers
35. Ringtones
36. White Papers
37. Product or service preview images
38. Early/exclusive access to a new website (also known as beta testing)
39. Teasers – short videos showing a new product or service or website preview
40. Third party coupons

a. Look for local offers to pass on, they cost you nothing but add value to your brand in the eyes of your audience
41. Screensavers

Fan Kits
42. Company logos
43. CSS files with company colours
44. Photoshop (PSD) files of product graphics for use on fan's websites
45. Photoshop colour palettes, with company and product specific colours
46. Product images
47. Deep links – URLs aimed directly at a product specific page

Geo-location Responses
48. Facebook Check-In deal
49. FourSquare, Gowalla or similar, offers and tips
50. Geo-tagging competitions

Audio
51. Upload audio files to Twitter via a dashboard such as Hootsuite
52. Upload audio to Facebook with a third party app
53. Record client testimonials
54. Guess the sound games
55. Product development personnel interviews
56. Conference speeches
57. Audio Blogs
58. News articles – always give credit to the source

Public Relations
59. Press releases – snippets and full files
60. Tear sheets – if you're mentioned in the media, link to the video or sound bite, or upload an image of your photo or article in the newspaper. (Copyright permission is required for photographing and publishing printed articles)

61. Press kits
    a. Press releases
    b. Logos for web, TV and print including guidelines on usage
    c. Media spokesperson photo

Surveys

Surveys can be public such as on a website or private, through an e-mail request. Incentives to complete a survey will drive more results but can be costly. Free giveaways such as Fan Kit materials are excellent incentives that cost only the production time and website bandwidth during the survey period.

62. Uses for a product
63. Product or service feedback
64. Thoughts on an event
65. Responses to a speech or specific advert
66. Brand or promotion sentiment
67. Requests for new ideas or features
68. Industry sentiment

Events
69. Event Announcement
70. Preparation photos and videos
    a. Marketing materials arriving in a lorry
    b. Staff struggling with advertising stands
    c. Boxed products
    d. Empty stand space
    e. Venue images – location of venue, location of stand at venue, food
71. Transport available to the venue
72. Local accommodation and other attractions in the area
73. Discounts from local retailers who will benefit from your venue attracting people to the area and will appeal to your target market
74. Parking Arrangements
75. Doors Opening
76. Early arrivals – the first people to attend

77. Staff and attendees
78. Candid images of the event – not professionally shot PR images.
79. Professional PR images – only release online after the media have published them
80. Photos of other retailers (non-competing) who may be attractive to your target market
81. Any famous faces – celebrities of any stature add weight to your brand when photographed standing next to your staff or stand
82. Packing up images
83. Happy event attendees / after event networking / partying

Comments

'Company' comments can be from the brand or an individual within the company. If an individual is to comment they must be signed up to a policy on speaking on behalf of the company. Even with this, it must be made clear their views are their own. This can be a double edged sword but the rewards are tremendous if you have a good writer.

84. Thoughts and views on industry news
85. Responses to customer feedback (always constructive)
86. Case studies
    a. Quote sources
    b. Include numbers – specific results are the key to a useful case study
    c. Include images (with permission and credits). Images can be related logos or indirect 'clip art'. A case study on how one company improved market lead time with an image of a clock beside it becomes surprisingly more readable than one without. Try it yourself to see the difference.
87. Book reviews
88. Movie reviews

Customer Service

The key to good customer service is consistency. Avoid random replies on a Saturday if your normal working hours are Monday to Friday, people will expect replies every Saturday if you do and complain if you fail to keep giving the same service.

89. Complaint Handling
    a. Work under a strict policy for what can and cannot be said
    b. If you deal with the complaint offline tell the people online what you did or they'll think you are ignoring other customers
90. Common enquiries
    i. Build up a list of Frequently Asked Questions and devote a page to them on your website or a Facebook tab to save time in the future
91. Apologies - apologise openly but don't offer discounts and giveaways publicly. They are a good way to appease a dissatisfied customer but if people think there is an easy route to free stuff via a quick complaint, you will be inundated.

Games

Online and social media games in particular don't have to be custom written behemoths of software engineering attracting millions of users. An 'Easter egg' hunt on your website for a graphic can produce equally good results if run correctly and include data capture.

92. Puzzles
93. Riddles
94. Easter Egg hunts – the egg can be anything such as a piece of text or an image
95. Arcade Games – lots of websites offer games you can embed into your website for free
96. Dingbats
97. Prize draws
98. Caption competition
99. Photo or video competitions
100. Text adventures
101. Custom built game software – expensive but with the correct data capture and interaction these can produce huge results in a short space of time

History

Historical information about your company builds an investment in your brand and gives people an insight into the development of your products and services.

102. Old photos
     a. Old premises
     b. Old staff profiles (especially where bad hair / outfits are showing)
     c. Old or out dated equipment
103. Previous TV adverts
104. Previous print ads or brochures
105. History of the company
106. Celebrations of key stages in the company's life
107. Awards
     a. Staff accomplishments
     b. Energy saving achievements
     c. Industry awards
     d. New contracts

Saying Thanks

People love to receive praise online, especially if they have been working in the background. If someone attends an event, makes a donation or simply mentions you in their blog it's an opportunity to say thank you.

108. Thank you for taking the time to visit my website and spend your hard earned money on my book. I hope it takes you at least one more step toward online profits.

9 BUILT TO SHARE

With our handful of followers starting to appear as Likes, Follows, Circle members, Connections and so on we quickly become fixated by what is known in the industry as vanity metrics. The Facebook beginner will get very excited to see their Likes break three figures with that magic 100. Online services abound that allow you to buy subscribers. For every type of subscription available there are list brokers offering instant subscribers to boost your vanity metrics. From their shiny web pages they proclaim the cheap, effective and instant gratification from obtaining hundreds, thousands and even millions of new followers all for the click of a button. In 2011 I tested these list sellers for Facebook and LinkedIn accounts. Everything they say is true. They will provide you with Likes from real people, connections who will invite you and send you a warm email welcome. My vanity metrics were boosted to astounding numbers and my page looked superb. Anyone visiting my Facebook page thought I was doing something amazing with hundreds of people joining every day. On the outside the service did exactly as it said it would, provide followers.

Upon reaching my goal of 800 Likes in a couple of days I continued with my twice daily updates providing the latest in marketing tips, news, blog posts and questions. Within two more days it became clear why vanity metrics are so named. My test page was compiled entirely of bought followers. My interaction levels were zero. Not only were these people outside my target demographic, they had absolutely no interest in my services. The majority were overseas and therefore outside my reach. Hundreds more were not in business of any kind and below eighteen so would have no use of my marketing services for some years to come. While I did receive the occasional Like on a comment my real metrics were so badly skewed as to be useless. Every metric was a percentage and as a percentage of the total subscribers, even a dozen Likes would have looked pitiful. All in all the purchasing strategy made the list sellers a few dollars but ultimately it destroyed my test page with empty followers.

So how do we build followers that are valuable, responsive and within our target market? Is it enough to build a small loyal following with only a few subscribers to our channels? Using the latest marketing channels doesn't mean we have to throw out all of our old marketing books. People remain the same, even if the platforms to reach them change.

Before social media, how did we treat our customer base when trying to win new business? When we wanted to attract more work what strategies did we try to make ourselves more appealing and attract bigger contracts? Often we used the 80:20 rule. 80% of your business comes from 20% of your clients. To attract more business we invited our clients to after work parties, networking events and handed out brochures and business cards. People enjoyed meeting people, they felt valued and passed on the goodwill and free hand outs. Social media hasn't changed this process. If in doubt, start with people. People will buy from people and people will share with other people.

Using our social media channels as an example, with only a handful of followers let's pretend they are our client base. If we want more followers we can treat them kindly, offer them free downloads, invite them to events and send them personal enquiries about their experience with your platforms. Each of these interactions will add value to their relationship with your brand. These 20% will start to attract the other 80% for you. By giving them materials they can share, pass on and use to add value to their own relationships with others they will start to promote your brand, purposefully and accidentally. It's easy to say there is no point in releasing lots of good content on our social media channels this week, only five people will see it. Those five people are known as early adopters. They want to know what your brand is doing. They are interested, i.e. invested, in your company. Your brand is a part of their lives, however small. Enrich that experience and they will reward you for it. Ignore it and you will lose them, forever.

One of the many advantages of social media is the ability to reuse and retain valuable information. While it is important to feed your early adopters good quality information, writing a detailed white paper that may only be seen by a handful of people can be an expensive use of time so it is important to maximise your content distribution.

Fortunately the Internet is filled with ways to share good content. Let's take our white paper as an example. After crafting our detailed white paper on the latest trends in digital marketing to mobile users in the UK and Ireland we have uploaded it to our website. Rather than send the link out on Twitter and Facebook with a short post about getting it free we'll take a paragraph and an image from the white paper and write a short blog post on the paper and our personal thoughts on the results. This takes the white paper from a factual document to a response on a factual document. Now we'll post the link to the blog article on Facebook and Twitter and invite other people's comments. This has four effects. Instead of a social media update and a white paper release, we have a white paper, a blog post, a social media update and an invitation to interact. Our handful of followers can now repost the link to the white paper or the blog. As you have already provided the link to the blog they are most likely to share that first but ultimately either share is good and your whitepaper will undoubtedly have all your contact links inside it anyway.

Now we start the additional process of making our whitepaper and blog post more publicly accessible. We start by sharing the links on bookmarking sites such as Reddit or Technorati. These can boost the readership of your content but also add to search engine optimisation. Bookmarking websites are just like the bookmarks in your browser except they are public. Many sites also allow you to vote on a bookmarked topic as being more or less interesting. Digg is a good example of shared content voted on by readers.

Next we take our whitepaper pages and break them into PowerPoint slides then upload them to a slide sharing website such as SlideShare. SlideShare allows you to share a presentation in a video format that people can scroll through or watch. The key element here is the embed function. You can take a snippet of code that holds your entire presentation, i.e. whitepaper, and embed it as a large video graphic on your website, LinkedIn profile, blog and other websites. This gives other bloggers and website owners the opportunity to embed your whitepaper as a useful, free piece of content on their sites making your content even more sharable.

The web is littered with great opportunities to share your content and quite often all it takes is a few minutes to reformat your material and submit it to a website but this process is what elevates your once seen content to highly shared material which quickly travels the web taking your brand and your social media channels with it.

By releasing your interactive content and inviting responses we start to build engagement with our current and soon-to-be followers. This system of sharing is also reciprocated and often sends useful information your way. This is not just valuable because new information is always useful but it's often surprising who sends you the information. Always look at where information comes from whether it's a link, a download or a blog post. Could the sender be in the market for your services? Is the platform hosting the content somewhere you should be sharing with? This flow of data is what builds a community around your brand and communities always have a voice.

Engaging with your community and listening to their responses is your goal as a social media marketer but fortunately the industry provides us with a wide range of free and paid for tools to assist us. Anyone hoping to maintain a sane level of interaction with their social media based audience must consider using a dashboard. Dashboards provide an overhead view of your channels all in one screen. They also open up accessibility to the many tools provided by the social media channels themselves but in a much more user friendly format.

HootSuite, SproutSocial, TweetDeck, RepKnight and Radian6 are all examples of social media dashboards. Prices range from free to thousands of pounds per year so you will have to base your decision on your expected return as well as your personal preferences.

Using our dashboard we can see all of our channels instantly, direct messages sent to us and most importantly, mentions of our name. These are conversations being had by people **about us** but not **to us**. In security terminology this would be known as back-chatter. Listening in on these conversations is perfectly acceptable in social media channels as long as you obtained the messages legally. Using a proprietary dashboard will ensure you're not breaking any privacy laws.

Figure 4- The Hootsuite Social Media Dashboard

The additional advantage of a dashboard, aside from the analytics (which we'll get to later) is the ability to schedule your messages. Rather than log in each day and send out an update, social media managers use a dashboard to release their messages in a timely, automated fashion. Don't confuse this facility with automated content. We are simply using the dashboard automation to send out our personally written posts at specific times.

10 SEVENTY-SEVEN KEYS AND ONLY TWO EARS

Content production and distribution is only one third of the equation yet it is easy to imagine that your message is where you should be spending the majority of your time.
The two remaining thirds are listening and analyzing. Listening is made simple with tools of the trade and should form the largest expenditure of your investment in social media.

Listening is largely an investment of time and not to be confused with reading analytics. Analytics will provide you with numbers that represent various response types but real listening is taking the time to understand what is being said inside your industry, about your industry and messages aimed directly at you.

Twitter will provide you with the simplest example of listening in on conversations by other people that are relevant to you and your industry. Go to www.twitter.com/search and enter any phrase or industry buzz word relevant to your business. Browse the Tweets of people from all over the world and you will quickly see how others perceive your industry, your industry brand and possibly even your individual company. Narrow your search to just the types of Tweet that are relevant to you and you have the option of saving that search for future reference. You can perform the same function inside many of the social media dashboards. Tomorrow you can refresh the search and start to build up a picture of the chatter around your products and services and those of your competitors.

On Facebook and less open channels we have to rely on the posts made on our page or we can follow the pages of our industry peers and read the comments posted there. Alternatively we can use the third party tools available that will listen to all of the social media channels, even those we don't subscribe to ourselves, and read the content being shared that is relevant to us.

Using what is known in the technology world as the 'Fire Hose', a number of companies provide a nozzle on all of the data being generated publicly by social media channels. Search for Gnip, InfoChimps or DataSift and have a look at their examples of how data is collected, packaged and redistributed for our analysis. Additional tools can then be subscribed to that give us the opportunity to scan all of the data out there for us to browse on demand. These tools all offer their own subset of functions such as categorization, sending out alerts based on specific keywords or phrases and varying levels of social analysis. One such tool is RepKnight, a social media dashboard known for its strength in sentiment analysis. Using a complex algorithm that measures intonation of written speech, i.e. social media comments, RepKnight will quickly categorize positive and negative material posted through the web. Graphs then demonstrate this sentiment overtime giving you a real time look at what people are saying right now.

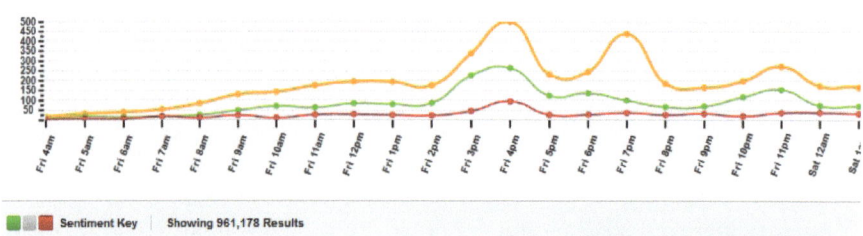

Figure 5 - RepKnight Sentiment Chart

While it's comforting to know what people are saying about you and your industry it's vital for the small business owner to be able to address these concerns quickly and effectively. Another feature of RepKnight is the option to view the original material posted and where it originated from giving us the reach to communicate with the users directly.

There are two sides to this level of response of course. It may be seen as 'big brother' watching every word written or as a proactive company seeking to understand its users and interact with them for the betterment of the product or service. How you handle those responses is ultimately up to you but it's important to be consistent, does your response type need included in your policy or will one person only address comments not directly sent to your customer service channels?

One alternative which fits comfortably between the two areas is 'indirect response'. When someone complains about a bottle leaking because of the shape of the lid it may not be appropriate to address the individual personally and suggest a different way of holding the bottle. A more measured response is to release a video showing how the bottle is supposed to be used. In more extreme cases where there is a large amount of negative publicity starting to appear, the release of several good news press releases along with a collection of videos which highlight the good points of your product will go towards quashing the story before it goes viral. These positive material releases will ensure searches for your product do not bring up bad publicity above the good in search results.

Law enforcement agencies use the same tactics in reducing the potential for hot spots and flare-ups at public events. For outside viewers it would be easy to imagine a large scale riot taking place when they perform a search on YouTube and see only the last ten videos posted depicting a burning car and stone throwing. By dissipating the videos with images of calm, a light police presence and good news surrounding an event there is less likelihood of the press picking up the story and thereby attracting more criminal elements to join in.

Another indirect tactic is to address the specific problem publicly. While it may not be appropriate to contact our soft drinks consumer personally, a product update notice about new lid designs coming soon or asking for feedback on the current design will give people the opportunity to respond constructively and by simply giving people the opportunity to provide feedback you will frequently find they are less concerned by the issue than they initially conveyed in their social media post.

While working in the security industry it always amazed me how often someone simply wanted to complain. They didn't want to fight or verbally abuse anyone, they simply felt their position must be heard in light of their concern over a product or service. By calmly giving them the opportunity to convey that message they frequently left a happier customer than before they had encountered an issue. Many in fact came back to apologize for their initial response. It was a common mistake by new people entering the job to mistake anger for a desire to fight and they would immediately become defensive creating an atmosphere that almost guaranteed a physical confrontation. This pattern repeats itself in the online world, especially where context is frequently invisible to both the end user and the company. It would be easy to become extremely frustrated by a bottle which leaked over your suit just before a meeting. An angry Tweet goes towards alleviating your anger in the hope the company will see it, especially when it's obvious there is a better way to construct the bottle lid.

For the company viewing the Tweet it is simply an angry person who's failed to hold the bottle correctly and now they're publicly abusing your company. The random person could not have known the manufacturing difficulties and costs involved in a better design but equally we could not have known the person was in their best suit and waiting for a job interview.

The key element here is 'the person'. If they are complaining about the product it is because they want a better one. They are not random or just a complainer, they are within your target demographic and they have a legitimate concern regardless of where they voice their response.

Taking the time to listen, understand and respond is where you will win customers and most importantly, retain them.

It is worth mentioning that not every single person who has a complaint about your product or service always has a legitimate claim to your time and efforts. People frequently use products for purposes they were not intended but fortunately for those people the 'Darwin Awards' are annually handed out.

11 THE MEASURE OF YOUR SUCCESS

A proper review of analytics has always been notoriously hard to interpret, time consuming and beyond the scope of any book smaller than a set of encyclopedias for the vast majority of business owners. A report in 2010 by Econsultancy and Lynchpin cited "Lack of Budget and Resources" accounting for 57% of businesses not having an effective online measurement strategy. 81% however was a combination of too much data, a lack of understanding, difficulty reconciling the data and a lack of trust in the numbers. (Respondents could choose up to three options, hence the non 100% total).

Google has addressed part of the problem through free Google Analytics which can be installed on the vast majority of websites in a few minutes. Over the years their analytics have increased in power and depth but to the new comer this is simply more options to confuse. Measuring social media is even more complex which leaves many people falling into the trap of vanity metrics.

It's easy to aspire to 500, 1000 or even 10,000 Likes on a Facebook page and in the early days it is important to get at least a couple of hundred people 'Liking' your page. The reason for this is co-branding. If you were to land on the Facebook page of a famous person or a well-known local sporting venue to discover they only had a dozen Likes, it is reasonable to assume you have landed on the wrong page, perhaps a fan page or someone trying to cash in on their brand name. This is one good reason to have a proportionate number of Likes on your page, Twitter followers or other vanity metric. The downside to chasing these numbers is their value. You can buy all the followers you want but their interaction levels will be virtually none. Attracting hundreds or thousands of Likes through competitions can be a great way to drive up followers but if they are simply prize hunters you are effectively buying Likes again, with little or no return.

So how do we build a follower base that has both value and spreads sufficiently fast to give us useful metrics that we can monitor and impress our marketplace with?
We go back to People. In the very early stages of testing our social media channels to determine how active our target market is on that platform we need to talk to people, actively engage them in conversation and give them reasons to tell their friends about us. So where do these people come from? We might start with a few friends possibly generating half a dozen followers but we quickly need to incentivize those people into sharing that conversation. Competitions are a great way to give people content they can share but you must create a competition that requires interaction. Simply following your pages is not enough (and in the case of Facebook will risk your page being deleted). Setting people challenges seems like a way to reduce the number of people entering and therefore reducing the number of followers you will gain but this is a perfectly good tactic. By narrowing the appeal of your competition you will give away a product or service to a select group of pre-qualified leads. The high value in any competition is not the short term exposure but the information gathered from the respondents. Their names and contact details is where you will recover the cost of the competition and build a customer base that you can engage with via your social media and sell to via your conversion channels over the coming months and even years.

The first question is how do we measure the value of our competition, or indeed any promotion we launch to build followers? Over time we will be able to gauge the interaction levels of our followers but this week and this month we need to demonstrate that our money is well spent and no busy manager wants to trawl through pages of data to find out.
The quickest way to evaluate the content you are producing is to give it a qualitative score.

This is a simple example using three videos. Videos can be made cheaply or professionally and there are cases for using a blend of both but in this case we used the cheaper 'home made' videos for improving our search engine optimization and to educate our target market.

Video 1 (figure 5) is a product demonstration. It aims to educate the audience about the services our company provides and at the same time help them understand the role of a social media manager when they hire one.

Figure 6 - Product Demonstration Video

Video 2 (figure 6) is a personal welcome to the company, talking about the brand, its values and aiming to connect with the consumer on a face to face basis.

Figure 7 - A Personal Introduction

Video 3 (figure 7) is a How-To video, also known as an 'instructable'. This is purely an education video that helps other people with their marketing strategy. Aside from a watermark or logo at the end of the video there is no selling involved.

Figure 8 - A How-to Video

Each of the videos will attract viewers but they each took different amounts of time to produce. Our first video required a few graphics and a short PowerPoint presentation, our second video took half an hour to write a script and a couple of minutes to shoot. Our last video took around two hours to successfully shoot the introduction and record the screenshots and voice over.

So here are the results of our three videos using some basic metrics:

20 views
5 likes
0 shares

200 views
40 likes
10 shares

Obviously the last video is where we should be spending our time in content production. Our how-to video generated 200 views, 40 likes and was shared 10 times. It's reaching a much bigger audience and will clearly bring in more business. If we believe the vanity metrics…

Going back to our value over vanity strategy we have now educated 200 people on one route to making money from Facebook and Twitter. If those viewers then decided they want a company to handle that process for them, they might return to us but most likely they'll try the strategy themselves then shop around. They were helped by us through a video on YouTube and probably went on to view a dozen more useful videos. Unless our video stood out in such a way that made our brand so amazing they could draw themselves away from YouTube to visit our page then we haven't really added very much to our sales funnel.

So should we only produce direct selling videos? We need a blend of different types of video, including the how-to. At the end of our video our happy viewer (we're assuming they were happy) is quite likely to have viewed more of our videos or even visited our YouTube channel. If they watched the video on our website they might click around some more to see what else they can find and if they watched it on our social media channel they might follow us in the hope of more useful content.

The blend of videos will attract bigger numbers through useful content, educate the viewers about our brand through personal appearances and walk them through the evaluation stage of the funnel through product demonstrations. To measure this process we give our videos a qualitative score of 1 to 10 based on how likely it is to bring the viewer closer to making a purchase:

Score: 10 (i.e. likely to sell our services)
50 views
20 likes
5 shares

Score: 5 (useful but not a sales pitch)
20 views
5 likes
0 shares

Score: 1 (educates but doesn't sell)
200 views
40 likes
10 shares

We can now calculate the true value of our video production and distribution. It would be easy to add a qualitative score to every piece of content we produce and while that's not a bad thing, do be careful not to get bogged down in generating an internal system that is more work than actually producing the content itself.

A simple quality score applied to time consuming or expensive processes such as video production is a quick and practical way to ensure you are producing a blend of content types and getting the best return on your exposure.

It would be safe assume there is a higher value in clicking on the Like button than simply viewing the video and likewise for sharing the video so we multiply those scores up. Here are the final results:

Score: 10
50 views
20 likes (x2)
5 shares (x3)
Total: 555

Score: 5
20 views
5 likes (x2)
0 shares (x3)
Total: 110

Score: 1
200 views
40 likes (x2)
10 shares (x3)
Total: 310

Reviewing the scores now with our qualitative totals we can see the first video actually produced a better result than our how-to video with 200 views.
It is worth stressing that giving your content a quality value is a simple process that can be quickly applied to your content production and will greatly boost your decision making process in what sort of video or other content to produce next. It is important to have a blend of content but it is

also important to understand the value of your content before you get led astray by the vanity metrics.

The next set of metrics to look at are the numbers provided by each of the social media channels. These vary dramatically from huge spreadsheets, for example from Facebook:

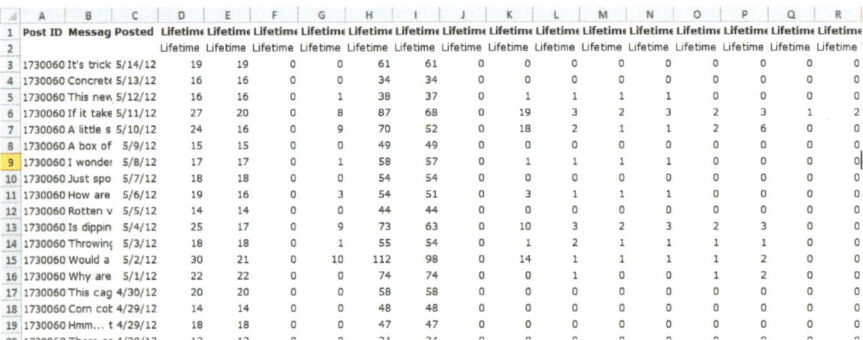

To Twitter, who provide almost none. Each platform provides its own help files and I've listed a number of these in the Appendix but there are common denominators in every channel.

The vanity metrics are usually proudly displayed somewhere for all to see such as Likes, Followers, Subscribers, Circles, Visitors and so on. One point which still frequently confuses people when looking at website statistics is Hits versus Visits. Visits, also known as Unique Visitors are the number of people* who have visited your page. Hits are the number of requests for pieces of content on your page with each piece of content representing one hit. For example, a simple web page with some text and four images is one page + four images = 5 hits. Be very careful when buying or selling advertising online when someone quotes their number of Hits. Unique Visitors with verifiable records of those visitors are what you really want to see.

*The accurate measurement is the number of unique IP addresses, i.e. computers, that have visited your page rather than people. It is assumed that each computer represents one person.

To measure our social media marketing we start with one metric: unique visitors.

How many of those visitors convert to sales is the first obvious question but as our sales funnel showed, there are a number of steps before anyone reaches the sales stage. What to look for next are the metrics which relate to each of those stages.

Here are our thirteen stages of funnel from both directions, also known as inbound and outbound. If you'll recall from the beginning of the book, the top down, or outbound is our marketing, the material we produce and distribute. The bottom half of the sales funnel, or inbound marketing is the material produced, shared and commented upon by the public.

Stage	What to Measure	Sample Metric
Marketing	Exposure	No. of channels
Awareness	Conversation Volume	No. of mentions
Interest	Subscriptions	Likes, Follows
Evaluation	Customer service enquiries; brand or product research	Enquiries via all communication channels; visits to portfolio pages or further product information
Commitment	Email sign up; brand advocacy;	Site registration (providing contact details); positive comments about your brand
Referral	Product specific enquiries, directly or indirectly	Product specific questions; requests for other users experiences
Sale	Journey to point of conversion, cost of journey, number of sales	Post purchase survey results; cookie tracking; purchases made on platform referred landing pages[1]
Referral	Source of referral; temperature[2]	Website analytics 'Referrers'; cookie

		tracking; pre-sales survey; product specific landing pages; customer referral incentives;
Commitment	Brand advocacy; early sign ups to offers	Positive posts about your brand; email sign ups or registration
Opinion / Evaluation	Enthusiasm; detailed questions	Speed of engagement; positive feedback; specific enquiries
Interest	Feedback on material posted	Likes, comments, retweets, replies, social bookmarking
Referred Interest	Followers not coming from direct marketing	Enquiries demonstrating a lack of product knowledge
Referral	'Virality' of marketing	Reach of message to people and platforms outside direct marketing channels
Social Media	Conversation volume	No. of mentions

[1] Landing page optimization is a vital way to measure the final sale. An online shop for example may have a single checkout but each product may have a page for each preceding link, for example a page demonstrating the product that is designed specifically for Facebook users. The link to that page can only be found on Facebook and nowhere else. That referring link to the checkout then provides you with a clear link between Facebook initiated purchases and website initiated. Be careful not to confuse this method with a single route to purchase. It is highly unlikely an individual will find your product on Facebook then not be influenced by content on multiple, additional locations.

[2] Referral temperature refers to hot or cold referrals. Cold referrals are not pre-sold on the purchase, i.e. they will form their own opinions on the

product with no positive third party influence. Hot referrals are normally recommendations from friends or other consumers or they have personal experience of the product or brand and therefore more open to making a purchase.

At first glance this may seem like an awful lot to measure and some of the measurements require technical knowledge to fully understand such as cookie tracking but don't shy away from measuring, it's the last vital action in a successful (money making) social media strategy.

To get into a simple routine of measuring success beyond vanity metrics record the 'Conversation Volume', i.e. the number of mentions. Search for your own brand or product once a week on each social media channel and on Google. Make a note of the total number of times you have been mentioned. Do it again next week and compare the figures. This is a very simple metric that will give you a feel for the activity of your brand in the marketplace.

Another very easy way to do this is with a dashboard such as Hootsuite or RepKnight where you can save searches and simply run them once a week. Within Google you can receive email alerts whenever your brand is mentioned on a web page which is a great way to monitor blogs (the blogosphere). It's free and available here: http://www.google.com/alerts TweetBeep provides the same service for Twitter: http://tweetbeep.com

Over time you will quickly build up an arsenal of key metrics which will assist you in the decision making process of where to market next, what sort of content to produce and who you will be targeting. It is this process that will give your business a clear, focused strategy that is both flexible to new channels and practical for busy managers.

12 WHAT TO DO NOW

You are now armed with a wealth of how-to information, anecdotal stories and social media case histories. To absorb all of this information instantly would be impressive, so below is a list of your next steps. It's a summary of all of the content in the book that should help you refer back to the key elements and get your social media marketing on track. Don't forget the resources in the Appendix and the downloads from the website. There is also more information on my marketing blog which is linked to from the website.

Hopefully you have found this book both useful and practical and I look forward to hearing about your social media successes.

- Step 1. Print off a copy of the updated sales funnel (see website).
- Step 2. Define your target market, look at your current customers, your competition's customers and products and services related to your business.
- Step 3. Compare your demographics to the social media channels – what's your potential reach in each channel?
- Step 4. Test the channels that don't have demographic numbers.
- Step 5. Choose a strategy for your channels, marketing, customer service, branding, education, a blend?
- Step 6. Define your policies for staff and consumers.
- Step 7. Engage your market, regularly.
- Step 8. Refine your messaging, plan and co-ordinate your content.
- Step 9. Inspire sharing, listen, interact.
- Step 10. Measure a little.
- Step 11. Measure a little more (while still sharing, listening and interacting).
- Step 12. Rinse and repeat.

APPENDIX

Social Media Dashboards
 Hootsuite – www.hootsuite.com
 SproutSocial – www.sproutsocial.com
 RepKnight – www.repknight.com
 Tweetdeck – www.tweetdeck.com
 Radian6 – www.radian6.com

Social Media Demographics
 www.facebook.com/ads
 www.linkedin.com/ads
 www.twittercounter.com
 www.youtube.com/yt/advertise/demographics.html

Social Media Policy Best Practice
 www.socialmedia.org

Copyright Free Images for Commercial Use
 www.publicdomainpictures.net
 http://office.microsoft.com/en-us/images/
 www.bestphotos.us
 www.ars.usda.gov/is/graphics/photos/
 http://images.fws.gov
 www.defenselink.mil/multimedia/
 www.nps.gov/archive/yell/slidefile/index.htm
 http://photolibrary.usap.gov
 http://phil.cdc.gov/phil/home.asp
 www.photolibrary.fema.gov
 www.nps.gov/archive/grca/photos/index.htm
 http://nix.nasa.gov

Website Accompanying this Book Including Free Downloads
 www.crackingsocialmedia.net

ABOUT THE AUTHOR

Michael Thompson has worked in more industries over the last fifteen years than most people will be aware of in their lifetime. From security roles in Northern Ireland to tracking game in South Africa, Michael has never been shy of adventure or risk. After teaching himself HTML and PHP he launched his own web design business in 2001. In 2004 he opened his first online business selling marine photography equipment to divers around the world and within one year was the largest supplier in Ireland. Within another year he had closed the business at a spectacular loss, taught himself debt management and started working his way back to profitability.

In late 2006 he joined Harrison Photography as the I.T. manager looking after an archive housing fourteen years of images and continuing to grow at the rate of 2TB per year. He quickly automated many of the tasks associated with managing the data, freeing himself up to join the photographers, working alongside the late John Harrison, one of Northern Ireland's most prominent press photographers.

Now working as a digital marketing consultant and tutor of the Chartered Institute of Marketing courses in Belfast, Northern Ireland, Michael provides social media training and digital marketing strategies to medium sized businesses and blue chips in the UK, Ireland and mainland Europe.

www.ingramcontent.com/pod-product-compliance
Lightning Source LLC
Chambersburg PA
CBHW041104180526
45172CB00001B/108